Hybrids of Plants
and of Ghosts

PRINCETON SERIES OF CONTEMPORARY POETS
David Wagoner, *Editorial Adviser*

JORIE GRAHAM

Hybrids of Plants and of Ghosts

PRINCETON UNIVERSITY PRESS
PRINCETON, NEW JERSEY

Library of Congress Cataloging in Publication Data will be
found on the last printed page of this book

Publication of this book has been aided by a grant from the
Paul Mellon Fund of Princeton University Press

This book has been composed in VIP Aldus

Clothbound editions of Princeton University Press books
are printed on acid-free paper, and binding materials are
chosen for strength and durability

Printed in the United States of America by Princeton
University Press, Princeton, New Jersey

Designed by Laury A. Egan

But he who is wisest among you, he also is only a discord
and hybrid of plant and of ghost.
—Nietzsche, *Thus Spoke Zarathustra*

For my mother and father

CONTENTS

IV

ACKNOWLEDGMENTS

Some poems have appeared in the following publications:

Antaeus: Ambergris
Pearls
A Feather for Voltaire
On Why I Would Betray You

The Georgia Review: Jackpot

Ironwood: Tree Surgeons
Strangers
Harvest for Bergson

The Nation: How Morning Glories Could Bloom at Dusk
The Chicory Comes Out Late August in Umbria
For My Father, Looking for My Uncle
Angels for Cézanne
Netting

The Paris Review: Mirrors

Ploughshares: In High Waters
I Was Taught Three

Poetry Northwest: The Way Things Work
Mother's Sewing Box
Girl at the Piano (It Begins, What I Can Hear)
Tennessee June

The Virginia Quarterly Review: Hybrids of Plants and of Ghosts
To Paul Eluard

Shenandoah: Whore's Bath

Agni Review: Now the Sturdy Wind

Missouri Review: One in the Hand

The New England Review: An Artichoke for Montesquieu

Paintbrush: Cross-Stitch

The Iowa Review: For Mark Rothko
The Geese

Water Table: Mind
The Slow Sounding and Eventual Reemergence Of
Syntax

ix

I

THE WAY THINGS WORK

is by admitting
or opening away.
This is the simplest form
of current: Blue
moving through blue;
blue through purple;
the objects of desire
opening upon themselves
without us;
the objects of faith.
The way things work
is by solution,
resistance lessened or
increased and taken
advantage of.
The way things work
is that we finally believe
they are there,
common and able
to illustrate themselves.
Wheel, kinetic flow,
rising and falling water,
ingots, levers and keys,
I believe in you,
cylinder lock, pully,
lifting tackle and
Crane lift your small head—
I believe in you—
your head is the horizon to
my hand. I believe
forever in the hooks.
The way things work
is that eventually
something catches.

names for the tree facing my window
almost within reach, elastic

with squirrels, memory banks, homes.
Castagno took itself to heart, its pods

like urchins clung to where they landed
claiming every bit of shadow

at the hem. *Chassagne*, on windier days,
nervous in taffeta gowns,

whispering, on the verge of being
anarchic, though well bred.

And then *chestnut*, whipped pale and clean
by all the inner reservoirs

called upon to do their even share of work.
It was not the kind of tree

got at by default—imagine that—not one
in which only the remaining leaf

was loyal. No, this
was all first person, and I

was the stem, holding within myself the whole
bouquet of three,

at once given and received: smallest roadmaps
of coincidence. What is the idea

that governs blossoming? The human tree
clothed with its nouns, or this one

just outside my window promising more firmly
than can be

that it will reach my sill eventually, the leaves
silent as suppressed desires, and I

a name among them.

WHORE'S BATH

But the water will not undress me, and where its coins on my body accumulate,
the sun builds its church, the soap its greenhouse.
They need remain empty.

Oh when will the whole become a permanent mirage?
Kneeling, I
can go abroad into my face, making both—the real and its proof—
disappear. What a fabric!

Yet what can it fashion, spirit unfastened to reveal
the blackest of urchins losing itself in its love of knots.
Lifting the pan, whitewater starts at the nape and disappears
into the waistline

absolving
each robing of skin
like the brazen descents of continents to water from the single idea
of their summit. The clean

is such a steady garment, such a perfected argument.
Where does it unfasten?
When I stand again I cast an exclamation mark onto the soil,
it is so adamantly

fragile. So believable.
What runs down my body now runs into other seasons than this
but the water is left to venture
round and round like a potential shadow, a suitor, though I

see nothing past the surface now, twisting my hair, a chord
interrupted. Where wind picks up,
crickets like rings
on fingertips . . . At the last

what I desire is
nostalgia for a moment different from another's moment, undressed,
clean,
all that you cannot give away.

AMBERGRIS

Because our skin is the full landscape, an ocean,
we must be unforgettable or not at all.

Squids that are never seen alive surface
to follow the moonlight on the water—anything

that flees so constantly must be desirable.
In doing so they run aground or are caught

by their enemy the whale. Sometimes fishermen
hang paper lanterns on the prows of skiffs

and row backwards towards land. It takes
such a long time to believe

in evidence.
Consider the broken moon over the waves,

the missing scent of moonlight
on salt water—eventually

pattern emerges. The giant squid
is rarely seen alive, but whalers often find it

dead in whales. There
it exudes the powerful fragrance,

its spirits—*Joy, Fly By Night, Green
Paradise*—always working towards

what must become the finished. Ambergris, what
was her name? it moves before me almost within reach—

jasmine, lavender, bergamot, rose . . .

TENNESSEE JUNE

This is the heat that seeks the flaw in everything
and loves the flaw.
Nothing is heavier than its spirit,
nothing more landlocked than the body within it.
Its daylilies grow overnight, our lawns
bare, then falsely gay, then bare again. Imagine
your mind wandering without its logic,
your body the sides of a riverbed giving in . . .
In it, no world can survive
having more than its neighbors;
in it, the pressure to become forever less is the pressure
to take forevermore
to get there. Oh

let it touch you . . .
The porch is sharply lit—little box of the body—
and the hammock swings out easily over its edge.
Beyond, the hot ferns bed, and fireflies gauze
the fat tobacco slums,
the crickets boring holes into the heat the crickets fill.
Rock out into that dark and back to where
the blind moths circle, circle,
back and forth from the bone-white house to the creepers unbraiding.
Nothing will catch you.
Nothing will let you go.
We call it blossoming—
the spirit breaks from you and you remain.

HYBRIDS OF PLANTS AND OF GHOSTS

I understand that it is grafting,
this partnership of lost wills, common flowers.

That only perfection can be kept, not
its perfect instances. Snap-

dragon what can I expect of you,
dress of the occasion?

So I am camouflaged,
so the handsome bones make me invisible.

It is useless. Randomness,
the one lost handkerchief at my heart,

is the one I dropped and know
to look for. Indeed, clues,

how partial I am to bleeding hues,
to clustering. Almond,

stone fruit,
you would be a peach, an apricot—

but see how close you can come without
already being there, the evening pulled in

at your waist, slipping over your feet,
driving them firmly into place,

the warm evening saying Step, anywhere you go
is yours, sweet scent in a hurry, to bloom is to be

taken completely—.
White petals, creaseless and ambitious,

may I break your even weave, loosen your knot,

and if I break you are you mine?

The almost invisible
shuttlecock at dusk
floats over the fine net,
coming to bloom in
the empty gardenia bush.
Not because happiness
exists, but because
it can be deduced
from continuities
such as these—yew
trees, dark windows
holding back dark sky,
white flower. Here
at the edges of belief,
the boundary the kites
have crossed breaking away,
it is what holds still
too long that belongs
to us. The gaps
between the trees
move more rapidly.
You can feel them
in your kite's crisp
desire the moment before
it leaves you. Above,
in the garden clouds,
home away from home,
tails drawn back in and
tucked into the pattern,
the gentle kites
find suddenly
what cannot hold them—cone,
cylinder, sphere and
signature like breath
scoring the pane
between us.

CROSS-STITCH

There is a cricket I can't find, trapped in this house, loud and lost
though thoroughly at home. He sings
when I turn the lights on.
Nothing is louder

than his perpetual failure
to recall just how he came here. Within our life
is another life, a second memory of the same event, where we
forget. Without,

we are able to listen to someone else's story, believe in
another protagonist, but within,
his presence would kill us.
In our best world, the absolute

fragrance of fully ready pears, becoming their portion of sunlight,
opens into us, arriving
by losing its way: Theirs is
another destination,

a form of pride
that blossoms into ours, taking its measure. In that world
of lost directions
the catalpa have dressed in their fringes for the single occasion

of our interest,
and the willows reach further than the soil to lock their fingers
with the weeds. Yet outside
the perfect arrivals of their green circuit,

anything can translate
its loss into ours. This cricket, for instance, finding the way
from there to here,
and finding the way to lose it.

STRANGERS

Indeed the tulips
change tense
too quickly.
They open and fly off.
And, holding absolutes
at bay, the buds

tear through the fruit trees,
steeples into sky.
Faith is where we are
less filled
with ourselves, and are
expected nowhere—

though it's better to hurry.
The starlings keep trying
to thread the eyes
of steeples.
It's hard, you can't
cross over. The skin

of the pear tree is terse
like the pear, and the acorn
knows finally
the road not taken
in the oak.
We have no mind

in a world without objects.
The vigor of our way
is separateness,
the infinite
finding itself strange
among the many. Dusk,

when objects lose their way, you
throw a small
red ball at me
and I return it.
The miracle is this:
the perfect arc

of red we interrupt
over and over
until it is too dark
to see, reaches beyond us
to complete
only itself.

DRAWING WILDFLOWERS

I use no colors, just number threes,
and though I know there are gradations I will miss, in this manner
    change
is pressure brought to bear, and then—
as if something truthful could be made more true—

the spiderwebs engraved on all successive sheets, flowers inhabited
by the near disappearances of flowers.
Having picked one
I can start anywhere, and as it bends, weakening,

ignore that.
I can chart the shading of the moment—tempting—though shading
changes hands so rapidly.
Yet should I draw it changing, making of the flower a kind of mind

in process, tragic and animal, see how it is rendered unbelievable.
I can make it carry *my* fatigue,
or make it dying, the drawing becoming
a drawing of air making flowerlike wrinkles of the afternoon,

meticulous and scarred.
Brought indoors and moored to vases, unwavering light, I can take
    my time,
though passage then is lonely, something high and dry and
gotten used to,

something noble.
A bouquet is another thing—purple lupine, crimson paintbrush, pink
forget-mes clash. One can try, in imitation,
indication by default—

a suggested real, though not the same, a difference
from which not enough is lacking.
Watercolors could achieve the *look* of it, two mapped but hostile
    lands
resigned to their frontiers—but it's an abstract
    peace, magenta meeting

14

crimson; crimson, scarlet.
But these in our fields, the real, the sheet of paper, the bouquet,
will not negotiate, and how I love
my black and white and the gray war they make.

II

MOTHER'S SEWING BOX

In an old cookie tin, because
things last longer
in the dark.
She needs to be left alone.
Here are saved
the bits of string
too small to save, the eyes
of the needles.
On the string
the knots are birds that sit,
that cannot leave. The buttons
are wheels. Assemble them,
these uneven machines,
and they say, *how much
for Effort*, or, *wait,
I've changed my mind,
I want to come along.*
To disobey
is to hide or to be
unmended. Maybe you'll find it,
she says after I've said
I don't have, didn't take,
her belongings.
The spools of thread
form a train. Swarms
of starling cry we are pins,
pins. We are going so fast.
*Maybe you'll
find it, maybe
you'll find it, lazy susan
got a black eye.* The needle,
covering its tracks,
makes a pattern
of its incisions, the pincushion
with its pocked body
snapped quills . . .
*and if she isn't gone
she lives there still.*

FOR MY FATHER LOOKING FOR MY UNCLE

The clues are everywhere.
Between the trees, small drafts that make the forest visible.
It takes forever to believe the dead are friendly.

We feel their unwillingness in the pines
motioning their needles in small reprimand.
In West Virginia they are marked with bouquets on the lawn;
at the end of each bouquet, a hand that can't let go,
and each in his own drawer at once hidden and found.

My father buried his brother's ashes here in a jar
with a bottle of rye.
Later, he didn't want him drinking alone.
Where did you go? Fall,

the trees go elsewhere,
leaving behind, with us, their heavier plumage, unfit for travel.
Look beneath the carpet of yellow leaves, or in
the fragments of the broken teacup still tasting of smoke.

Christmas, we opened the calendar windows, one
each day, until we believed there was another indoors,
assiduous, free, a small community, a dream with shutters.

THE CHICORY COMES OUT
LATE AUGUST IN UMBRIA

Fall, there is open season
on songbirds.
You eat them whole.
Late August
they sing all night
and line up on the wires
as if to make of their bodies
small notes;
a very simple song theirs,
almost a straight line
like the men going home,
looped strings
over their backs,
their dogs faithless
but willing
to be owned
(or is it *because*?).
You cannot enter
says the birdsong;
you cannot enter says
the thirteenth century;
you cannot, says the sky
dropping and forcing you
to look away. The chicory
comes out late August,
purple heads
like grass skirts
covering what I
used to take for
nakedness.
Because they are wild
they are useful.
Once upon a time,
they say,
she got him after all.

SYNTAX

Every morning and every dusk like black leaves
the starlings cross,
a regular syntax on wings.
The gravestones lean, each
more or less than its neighbor,
as if to find
a whole view—
not unlike the way, in a crowd,

we move to exclude others
without degrading them,
or how we wish, in conversation,
to step aside without stepping back;
or in desire.
They say the eye is most ours
when shut,
that objects give no evidence

that they are seen by us.
Perhaps we move then
to watch a tree stay still
or move the other way from us, to feel
not so much its distance as its loss.
When the pond froze
we carved our names on its delicate surface
jumping from letter to letter

to hide our tracks.
I misspelled mine out of excitement,
seeing it so big and knowing it would last
till the first thaw
threaded the water
like a needle.
Spring we hunted bullfrogs.
We caught the ones that sang.

TREE SURGEONS

Like feelers off into last night's dream, out beyond the screens,
they move in approximate circles around my neighbor's elm.
Gleeful performers,
they know they belong here,

drawing their large bows, toothed strings,
across each branch with great discrimination.
What crooked instruments! And yet
symmetry governs,

theirs an elm of two nests, two squirrels,
a skinny elm of split decisions.
How evenly it is rid of itself, tree of no nuance, no preference,
of no cardinals loading red

onto the sunny half. My neighbor sweeps the porch.
It is taking longer than expected.
There is no *temporarily* she thinks.
I think she secretly admires the dust, how evenly each grain

falls into place, as if grown upward
from the meaning of the thing itself—davenport, commode—
more even than forgiveness,
better even than the clean slate of *you were only dreaming*.

The tree is almost done.
Offspring to mainline, now everything is sure where it began.
My window splits in two—
her elm, then mine, shaggy,

headed some other way.
Like one who leaves, and the other who remains, they are
each other's constant, sullen victims
and yet safe

from one another.
The daylight has gone although we are not yet in darkness.
I stand at my window. The light draws in.
I cannot say why, but they are much too safe from one another.

NETTING

My father would have saved us, had the occasion of fire arisen.
Sundays, each at our post,
we practiced—
his fine network of hoses lacing into perfect

webs. So much water,
and each of us a knot we felt so safe in manning.
I never really understood the underpinnings, miraculous nation
beneath the smooth lawn—

a private patriotism.
Nothing again was ever as dangerous, as vulnerable. I know of father
less than I imagine, but in the end
all that we can know of anyone

is what we promised them. I know, therefore,
that fire is something we can catch, unwittingly, like cold,
and that these tiny roads
woven round and round our property like a spare set of roots,

is what we really are—a shadow map, a future kept alive by
met commitments.
And at those junctions, the world seems as private as public,
a well-kept secret

kept by all. Just as, deep in a cave, life can survive
only because of forms of life outside that will persist
in entering. So . . .
water to save us, and

profound curiosity—casting and trawling and building a surface
able to truly hold us,
like gossip, or the smell of lilacs, or an overheard song: soon
everyone has caught it.

JACKPOT

Halfway through Illinois on the radio
they are giving away jackpots.
I can hear them squeal as they win.
Luck in this landscape lies flat
as if to enter the ground and add to it as well.
You can see its traces, milkweed caught in the fences,
the sheen on the new grass
that could be sunshine or white paint.
But the brushstroke is visible.
We wouldn't believe anything we saw without it—

the brown, the green, the rectangle, the overpass.
I believe now that sorrow
is our presence in this by default.
In a little while I hope there will be shadows,
the houses and these trees trying to bury half of themselves.
This could be your lucky day,
the day the roof is put on the house
and the willows once again resemble trees
and the bridge falls in, making the river once again
sufficiently hard to cross.

HARVEST FOR BERGSON

Last night I watched the harvest moonrise. There were moths
trapped in with me. Hear them tap like fingertips
on walls and windowpanes. For moonlight
blurs the facts,

its shade not keen or rational like that of sunlight
seeking to capture the nature of its subject;
it seeks, rather, to let it go,
to show what it is not . . .

Because it is what is not animal in us, the best intentions
    we still have
at the moment of perception: to see it all.
Then we grow hot, tragic and fleshed
with intellect,

dividing. The world we live in
is going to change, to more than disappear.
This is the light that blinds you by degrees
that it may always feel like sight. This is the world

in profile, medieval,
the landscape gathered up into the face, the foreground;
and if the foreground sways
it isn't to awaken us, ever so gently; no, it means for us
    to go

to sleep, perspective drawing in like peasants gathering
    within the city walls
when war is imminent. The distance, its fields,
growing baroque, then wild

then dry. And those that, squinting, will peer out over
    the moonlit walls tonight,
can't quite make out the empty fields, which one
is theirs; it slips their mind. . . . This is what dies
    not in duration
but in time.

FLOODING

Just rain for days and everywhere it goes it fits,
like a desire become too accurate
to be of use, the water
a skirt the world
is lifting and
lifting

like a debt ceiling.
And everywhere you go you are the land between the lakes,
the stroke of luck which has the world
it splits in two
for wings.
Our ponds

are almost joined. How much more than what we wished for
must we get? How much more than plenty? Too much
of a good thing,
too much,
the head becoming
crown . . .

And how this cinderella land is in full dress, ballooning,
overriding all
ramifications, her gown
lifting and lifting
from marsh
to pond

to the lap of the lawn.
Oh the long-legged guest!
And where she comes from
I can't say, although I think it's from the peaks of new
desires to these
our living-

rooms where love
is turning out the lights when others do, a curfew we
would take
for sails. What is it
must be given back
before it

disappears?
The land between the lakes
is growing thin.
Turn out the lights, I think, or water will.

A bird re-entering a bush,
like an idea regaining
its intention, seeks
the missed discoveries
before attempting
flight again.
The small black spirit
tucks in its wings,
softest accordion
whose music is
the perfect landing,
the disappearance
into the dangerous
wintered body
of forsythia. Just as
from time to time
we need to seize again
the whole language
in search of
better desires.
If we could only imagine
a better arc
of flight; you get
just what you want.
And see how beautiful
an alphabet becomes
when randomness sets in,
like mother tired
after disappointment,
and keeping us
uninformed—the man
walking away whom we
want to recall
and in whom we invest

the whole explanation.
One in the hand,
one in the mind,
how clearly you know
what you have, how clearly
what he'll want to do, and do
when you let go.

AN ARTICHOKE FOR MONTESQUIEU

Its petals do not open of their own accord. That is our part,
as the whisper is the hand we tender
to the wish, though each
would rather rule the field. What remains
is the heart, its choke a small reminder to be mindful
lest we go too far
for flavor. These are the questions
its petals part in answer to: where
is God? how deep is space? is it inhabited? The artichoke
is here that we imagine
what universe once needed to create it,
penetrable jewel;
what mathematics.
And then, now,

when the earth is no longer the world, it offers
a small believable cosmology:
each tiny leaf an oar
in the battle where each pulled his own; and the whole
the king himself, tiered like his crown or the multitude
laughing. The mind meets the heart
on such terrain as this, where each
can give in to the other
calling it victory,
calling it loss—
a no man's land where each of us
opens, is opened, and where
what we could have done locks to the very core
with what we have.

PENMANSHIP

Beyond the margin, in the mind, the winner gets it right,
while here the *l*'s proceed in single file,
each a large or smaller eye.
What heaven can be true
when its permissions
vary so? The page

is turned. Try it again. Each page a new decor, as here
the *f*'s so many shut umbrellas on
an empty beach, the waves the *s*'s make unable to link up,
reach shore, and this
a greenhouse, rows and rows and I
can't ever pick
the one I want,

and this the desert we'd reclaim,

and these the flooded lowlands, topsoil gone downstream, the ocean
flashing her green garments, many-stemmed and
many-headed,

and this our frigid school of twenty-six now swimming up
stream, swimming down, made to try
and try again,

and oh their desire, one by one, is for normalcy, marriage,
these labials and gutturals narrowing their aim,
shedding the body for
its wish, a pure idea, a thought as true as
not true, water

lilies, water-
striders. . . .

TO PAUL ELUARD

Farewell to the caterpillars standing in minks
in front of the Opera.
Nobody knows if they wait, if this is patience.

Farewell to the clocks fingering their wedding rings,
the murmuring moon,
farewell

to public appetite.
The seven headlengths of beauty have been cut off;
we are putting them back. In the end

the world is more like a person than not
and we are dust
only compared to what escapes us.

The professors of ethics are gathering in the meadows,
tears in their nets.
Butterflies teach us to see meanings vanish.

Not one gets away.

III

FRAMING

Something is left out, something left behind. As, for instance,

in this photo of myself at four, the eyes
focus elsewhere, the hand interrupted mid-air by some enormous,
sudden,
fascination.

Something never before seen has happened left of frame,
and everything already known
is more opaque for it.
Beyond the frame is why

the hydrangea midsummer will go no further, though it continues,
why this century, late and turning,
turns away; beyond
is where the story goes after all the knots are tied, and where

the insects meet in order to become
the grand machine they are the perfect parts of; beyond
is what the wind
leans towards, easy as can be, the sheep

we have already counted,
the world too large to fit.
Within, it would have been a mere event,
not destructive as it is now, destructive as the past remains,

becomes, by knowing more than we do.

FOR MARK ROTHKO

Shall I say it is the constancy of persian red
that permits me to see
this persian-red bird
come to sit now
on the brick barbecue
within my windowframe. Red

on a field made crooked
as with disillusion or faulty
vision, a backyard in winter
that secretly seeks a bird. He has
a curiosity
that makes him slightly awkward,

as if just learning
something innate, and yet
there is no impatience,
just that pose of his
once between each move
as if to say, and is *this* pleasing?

When I look again he is gone.
He is easy to imagine
in flight: *red extended flame,*
I would say, or, *ribbon*
torn from a hat
rising once

before it catches on a twig,
or, *flying painted mouth*
but then how far
have we come?
He could fly now
into a moment of sunlight

that fell from the sun's edge
ten thousand years ago,
mixed in with sunlight
absolutely new.
There is no way to understand
the difference. Some red

has always just slipped from
our field of vision, a cardinal
dropping from persian to magenta to white so slowly
in order that the loss
be tempted,
not endured.

THE GEESE

Today as I hang out the wash I see them again, a code
as urgent as elegant,
tapering with goals.
For days they have been crossing. We live beneath these geese

as if beneath the passage of time, or a most perfect heading.
Sometimes I fear their relevance.
Closest at hand,
between the lines,

the spiders imitate the paths the geese won't stray from,
imitate them endlessly to no avail:
things will not remain connected,
will not heal,

and the world thickens with texture instead of history,
texture instead of place.
Yet the small fear of the spiders
binds and binds

the pins to the lines, the lines to the eaves, to the pincushion bush,
as if, at any time, things could fall further apart
and nothing could help them
recover their meaning. And if these spiders had their way,

chainlink over the visible world,
would we be in or out? I turn to go back in.
There is a feeling the body gives the mind
of having missed something, a bedrock poverty, like falling

without the sense that you are passing through one world,
that you could reach another
anytime. Instead the real
is crossing you,

your body an arrival
you know is false but can't outrun. And somewhere in between
these geese forever entering and
these spiders turning back,

this astonishing delay, the everyday, takes place.

NEW TREES

For long it seemed nothing could be made again of these lean branches,
seamless, eyeless. Who
would have ever known there were so many exits

and that vanity could be regained from any one of them?
In that sleep how the chapters of reason
must have seemed accomplished

like so many brilliantly dissembled butterflies or the flames
mysteriously tucked into the delicate veins of pitch.
Looking at them now, every leaf

waving the others in, there is no way to imagine how
two such maps could ever overlap. And yet
it is what leaves the body after strictest exile there

that we believe in—bigger, so much fuller than the imagined
tree or the kernel of its definition. Tree
in which all that crossed the mind and all that slipped it find

a home and just reward,
in which the present keeps on breaking and is not turned away
by shores because they also break. And where each firm beginning

reaches its precarious destination at the tip,
giddy and unable to ascertain whether, having been attained,
it is instrument

or cause. From such we emerge, ours
a violence done to that stark line drawing *before* strictly to *after*
and from which we break over and over, branching as far

as we can conceive, each image
of ourselves growing increasingly identical like these leaves,
and waving like the mirage waves to keep our eyes from ever letting go.

ON WHY I WOULD BETRAY YOU

Because this is the way our world goes under: white lies,
    the snow,
each flake a single instance of
nostalgia. Before you know it
everything you've said
is true. The flakes

nest in the flaws, the hairline cracks, the stubs
    where branches
snapped—only unbroken lines, unwavering,
for building on. How easily our tracks
are filled. How easily
we are undone,

knowing the events
without the plot: caution and light and the odor of skin
    threading
the secret, a loom. What will happen?
What I do
in betrayal

is play at being small, the body a protectorate I can
    win back
at will; is alter the rules
in the pattern,
what happened.
It snows

like there is no tomorrow, the world growing younger
in her new attire. Who wouldn't love to render
her white lies to their flawlessness like this,
in brushstrokes
dagger true,

yet kind. For is it not true, this smooth new skin,
were we not also good? Each indiscretion
a caress of faithlessness,
a feather to touch
you by.

MIRRORS

For some of us the only way of knowing we are here at all, going
across and going down,
exquisitely temporal though at no point believable; fragile; tragic.
The mirror redeems

the desire to wish,
what we cannot see of ourselves staring back with its most accurate
        face.
The closer you come
the less believable—

life-size that dangerous democracy that will destroy its subjects.
Lookalikes, miniatures,
as in the world of pine, are stabs at freedom:
this limb twisted impossibly, that height not naturally achieved,

achieved. Or,
taking the lodgepole: in the clearings
their maps are unreadable, carrying their off-centeredness
        with vanity,
true love,

slow and doubling like ideas not yet come to term—but stubbornly
growing thick and burying themselves
in themselves
While in the forest,

the modest chemistries of need force all of them to grow cleanly
identical, histories
where only present tense survives,
the lower limbs all shed in compromise—as if in such a crowd

being overlapped and overlooked were being free . . .
Too many arrows
for identical hearts,
unwavering, unvarying, every one a hero, a mind

made up. What industry.
What will we become from lack of uselessness. What will we become
without that acute, fancy love—
branch off my own tree bent back to taunt and almost look alike.

MIMICRY

The other woman,
how I envy her,
a sort of Canada
to this confusion.
Its evergreens
are blue,
a protection
other than hiding—a woman

with time on her hands. Here
the trees turn yellow
without each other's knowledge
or help. Canada,
whose side
are you on, waiting
for yours—saffron,
jonquil, madder

and amber. The blue
evergreens
with their oblique needles
can wait forever;
they have lost
the small particular faces
of their instruments. In Canada
the eyes miss the background

and the fore. *Remember*
the long heavy pods of the locust, late August,
on the trimmed lawn,
small building materials
awaiting an idea?
Between the islands,
islands of water, trees.
Any interruption

invents them again. When a forest
burns, the mind
feels compelled to say
I did it, I must have
done it. In the water,
king's yellow, paris yellow,
gold. *Oh*
you could have.

SELF-PORTRAIT

After fresh snow I'll go up to the attic and look out.
My looking is a set of tracks—the first—
a description of the view
that cannot mar it.
Again and again
I trip across it,

terrain impregnable
yet yours for the sighting.
Eye-level in the world
something difficult in disappearing from our lives, something critical
like emphasis
or the blue

deep-grooved river currents now reduced to pattern
in the ice. While from up here
it seems less small a thing
to keep each to our side,
and everything
keeps trying

to reach the sky. I want to change for you,
though it would be by trying to stay the same.
A child, I thought the music
was the track the needle
cut, each time, anew
into the black

where it's still night and no one knows yet it has snowed.
Such solitary work,
this breaking ground
that will only reclaim itself.
Yet how I loved it,
returning the arm,

striking out anew, time and time again, and knowing all along
the circuit would not shut
and the start
elude the end
for every single note along the way.

GIRL AT THE PIANO

It begins, what I can hear, with the train withdrawing from itself
at an even pace in the night although it always seems
to withdraw from us.
Our house almost continues

in its neighbors, although the thinnest bent and wavering fence
keeps us completely strange.
Perhaps it is a daughter who practices the piano, practices
slow and overstressed like the train, slow and relentless

like the crickets weaving their briar between us and growing
    increasingly
unsure of purpose. These three sounds continue, and I
alongside them so that we seem to stand
terribly still. Every change

is into a new childhood, what grows old only the fiber
of remembering, tight at first like crickets and ivories,
crickets and train,
then slackening

though always hanging on to the good bones of windowframes and eaves
and white columns of the porch
in moonlight. Like taffeta, the song,
though not yet learned, is closer to inhabiting her hands

and less her mind, ever closer to believing
it could never have been otherwise. Your sleep beside me is the real,
the loom I can return to when all loosens into speculation.
Silently, the air is woven

by the terribly important shuttle of your breath,
    the air that has crossed
your body retreating, the new air approaching. See,
transformation, or our love of it,
draws a pattern we can't see but own. Like the pennies we pushed

into the soil beneath the pillowy hydrangea, pennies
that will turn the white flowers blue,
or the song I finish past her, the completely learned song
like my other self, a penny slipped next to the heart, a neighbor.

MY FACE IN THE MIRROR TELLS A STORY
OF DELICATE AMBITIONS

And yes it is a personal event, this flowering each time
    I look again; and no
it is not my portrait. Rather

see it as a granted wish, or, further, as who wished for it
in its silver room

where exit is blocked and it must turn back on its tracks,
    my tracks. And so,
this morning once again find

something more gathered and tucked; something devoted,
seductive. It is trying

to capture the true likeness of its subject, and I
need keep an eye on its attempts. For who

is it after, after all, face
inhabited by self as rock by lichen, blistering with motive?

At the last, the lichen, with its fancy scenarios, tentative heroes,
dries and blows away, although

whatever it be growing on—rock or bone—receives, for keeps,
the imprint of its delicate crusade, receives

the whole idea, the wish itself, down to the smallest
coded message, down

to this mirror, this morning, where the crusting features of
the moment begin

to press and leave, as in a bas-relief, the only true accounting of
this particular campaign,

this victory.

STILL LIFE

Beyond the windowframe, two wintered maples overlap sufficiently
to weave a third, a tree
all boundaries,
more opaque for the doubling,
and indivisible enough

to hold us,
like the body.
Beyond the windowpane, still weather
orders the world as though expecting thought, a premonition
of the real

in the still.
For at the windowpane
we are the heroes
leaving home to journey out over the visible, that trusty fabric,
and are the heroines

staying behind.
Sometimes a squirrel
will travel back and forth between the two trees thin as scaffolding—
small leaps like stitches
until their separation is

firmly repaired.
The shadow tree, the sum,
is home, it seems to me, a place where we were overcome and
overcame, the tree where each,
through the other, reaches

as far as it is possible
without trespass,
without diminishment—a darker tree, like the body to its wings,
a holding pattern
over this world

where to stay behind
when you go abroad
is to know how still the spirit really is that threads us.

IV

HOW MORNING GLORIES COULD
BLOOM AT DUSK

Left to itself the heart continues, as the tamarind
folds its leaves every night and the mimosa,
even in perpetual darkness, opens and shuts
with the sun.

It is moved by such delays:
cat's-ears open at six, african marigolds, lilies
at seven, at eight the passionflower.
Its light awaits the souls of the living, its birds

for the branches to unfold in song;
the end of its year awaits each noon the opening
of the chicory of the meadow, and its meadows
imagine other sleepless flower beds.

If there is another world, then this is it:
the real, the virtual, the butterfly
over the evening primrose.
The error involved is minimal, it can be corrected:

the blue of the sky
is due to the scattering of sunlight
on its way out of the sky.
But no one said how slow, how willing.

IN HIGH WATERS

Quartered, cleaned, this beautiful black wire looped and knotted
through the skin, the squash hung on the porch.
All September they puckered, cracked. Then they were dry.
They clicked a little when the wind

made its way past them: hollow sounds, almost pleasing—cupped hands
clapping a bit for themselves when we weren't looking.
November I drew them.
They had stopped changing.

I drew them landlocked. Canyons.
They scorned the rivers that had abandoned them.
Four phases of some moon, I drew them. Four rowboats run around.
Four, leashed to their piling, nudging each other

from time to time. Four sails
learning to quarter wind, gather way—what cunning, what incredible
patience! We brought them indoors to a large nail
in the kitchen. I drew them again, four ships in a rice-paper storm,

four rocks narrowly avoided by the sailor who,
thanks to them, finds his way home.
Four sailors' memories of the same girl. Now
you would cook them. Soaked in water, salt, they would plump up.

How nice to have things out of season. Summer squash
caught in our winter, there is snow outside
like you would not believe.
Whole trees are buried beneath waves, becalmed. The world

is everywhere able to flow into itself without damage
or confusion. Something we don't know is complete without us
and continues. On the other side
of the ocean, four dark sails joining to becoming black

granite cliffs buckle over the water's end,
protecting this finest of erosions. Rosemary. Thyme. You
quarter onions. I cannot tell you now—you are so pleased—but I
don't believe you should try to bring them back.

OVER AND OVER STITCH

Late in the season the world digs in, the fat blossoms
hold still for just a moment longer.
Nothing looks satisfied,
but there is no real reason to move on much further:
this isn't a bad place;
why not pretend

we wished for it?
The bushes have learned to live with their haunches.
The hydrangea is resigned
to its pale and inconclusive utterances.
Towards the end of the season
it is not bad

to have the body. To have experienced joy
as the mere lifting of hunger
is not to have known it
less. The tobacco leaves
don't mind being removed
to the long racks—all uses are astounding

to the used.
There are moments in our lives which, threaded, give us heaven—
noon, for instance, or all the single victories
of gravity, or the kudzu vine,
most delicate of manias,
which has pressed its luck

this far this season.
It shines a gloating green.
Its edges darken with impatience, a kind of wind.
Nothing again will ever be this easy, lives
being snatched up like dropped stitches, the dry stalks of daylilies
marking a stillness we can't keep.

THE SLOW SOUNDING
AND EVENTUAL REEMERGENCE OF

this whale, this valentine. Yours.
Your patience on parade. *Where is your quiet*
you said, for I can't hear
the oblique messages, the discords
your listening
is code for. And oh you are willing

to wait forever,
while the day is so quick and the noise, the volatile noise,
such a ladder. To hell
with installments, implications, slow
assimilation. Let's
buy it all. But you

are willing and waiting,
and at its soft core, this knowing nothing
about everything, I imagine
a slow pulse like that of sand in rock, and rock
in vein, though this vein
you travel—silk thread to its immense

whale eye—
does not begin its work, its tapering to dry. And yet
the patience of the visible
is the invisible—
Jack's beanstalk awaiting its accident, money
its palm. You go deeper

and deeper. From the surface, I
imagine what's beneath as vaguely heart-shaped, blue,
awaiting definition, roots.
You go deeper.
It could happen anytime, this blue that opens—
no decoy this, no trial run for you,

ambassador of absolutes
beached here among the relatives.
You forage. I finger the waiting. Each to our alibi.
It is the way
we celebrate, it is love, the way tomorrow finds us.
It could happen any time.

THE NATURE OF EVIDENCE

In winter the onset of day lingers all day,
the frozen vines of bittersweet have their mantilla drawn
over the bushes stiff as combs,
a marriage

the slightest growth would snap.
And the roses are happy trapped in their passage,
and the final wishes of the squirrels have been left
like necklaces over this still
and absolutely willing
nape—

they've all arrived someplace by now. Indoors,
our tracks are merely different:
what concerns us is luck,
whose turn it is.
Sometimes you

will take my clasped hands into yours,
wonderful double entry
that does not try to hide
how our two perfect sets of prayers

cannot be joined.
And even though I know how at all times, outside, beneath the still,
the fecund is preparing
its embodiment,
its escape,

how I would like to catch the world
at pure idea—although, as with my profile, I,
turning to it, find
only myself again,

and, no, it's not enough to understand
it's there because it's gone.

MIND

The slow overture of rain,
each drop breaking
without breaking into
the next, describes
the unrelenting, syncopated
mind. Not unlike
the hummingbirds
imagining their wings
to be their heart, and swallows
believing the horizon
to be a line they lift
and drop. What is it
they cast for? The poplars,
advancing or retreating,
lose their stature
equally, and yet stand firm,
making arrangements
in order to become
imaginary. The city
draws the mind in streets,
and streets compel it
from their intersections
where a little
belongs to no one. It is
what is driven through
all stationary portions
of the world, gravity's
stake in things. The leaves,
pressed against the dank
window of November
soil, remain unwelcome
till transformed, parts
of a puzzle unsolvable
till the edges give a bit
and soften. See how
then the picture becomes clear,
the mind entering the ground
more easily in pieces,
and all the richer for it.

NOW THE STURDY WIND

Now the sturdy wind is, more than ever, useful. It pulls
each reluctant hem of greenery from what it has got stuck on: air,
the blue between
the branches.

Leaves would otherwise remain, it seems, like so much currency,
out of date, still clinging to
a value presumed absolute.
Everything goes.

Everything goes in this wind, turning and twisting, seeking
in every seed
to be windborne, reborn,
in every leaf and stem and runner and the very smallest

flared buds off the lilacs.
And yet the weeds, what an example they set, here, where salvation is
to be released forever from
this thickset world—heal-all and speedwell,

devil's trumpet and deadnettle—how they return
always to the same, the one, adventure.
Can we say we really wish for more?
The wind's digression is

a magnificent outing, but all arguments cannot subscribe to it.
Some, like these deep-seeded weeds,
stand very still
and wish for us to do the same—a present tense at the heart
of the wind

in which we are
ready to go where everything goes and yet forever suddenly
distracted by
the beneficial undershoots of cattails,
the asters the songbirds need.

LOURDES: SYLLABLES FOR A FRIEND

So this is the weakness of the flesh, the urges
become wistfulness of mind; and here
the former cured
care for the hopeful,
each awaiting
total remission,
to be so absolutely

seen. And to be clean is to walk from here to there,
to overlook this world at will. So here
at her mouth, Saint
Bernadette who saw
no visions, they
await her hunger,
rows and rows of limbs and wheels

and independent second clocks—a twisted vine-
war like the kudzu, May, over the stands
of birch; each breathing,
each different hope,
interweaving like
the incandescent
tubework, oils, acids and clear

saline solutions. Nothing here is sweet that is
not also acrid. And the eye that offends
is the eye you can see through,
through which you are
seen. A miracle
would seem to be
what builds itself

in spite of us—white cells gone mad or syllables be-
coming thought. And these, the former cured,
are in more of a hurry
than the sick. They know
unfairness could
strike anytime,
that hallowing, that change of mind.

THE AFTERLIFE

In the afterlife there is shade in the weave of severe
sunlight. Fatigue
is a kind of joy.
In some of us the afterlife loosens feature after feature

as if this life were held in bones, boundaries that melt
easy as the claims
of progress. Its loneliness is jazz.
The afterlife affords us sudden clearings in the woods,

succinct transitions in the argument. And it exacts a church,
divides us perfectly among the pews.
Perfectly we face
all the same way, believing

we overlook nothing.
It faces only out
to the dour sadness of the aspen going suddenly heavy
on themselves, pastel petit-point

to no avail. How could they have emerged from such stark maps
in which only the road taken
survived? In this afterlife
blossoming sustains the linear, the chainlink of new ivy does

the sagging barn. Our houses also entertain it, each
in its separate maze;
the grass portrays it tapering and eager to remain
untouched. It is the mainsails

awaited by the lightning-stricken pine,
the point imagined by the mind that it may vanish, enter.
The afterlife is electricity
communicated

wholly, nothing
lost in process. Not the gravestones placed
as bookmarks in the earth—as if
we could lose our place—not us as we keep on reading.

PEARLS

Here the world, in fall, engenders mast that it may tempt
the grazing barnyard animals
from domesticity.
Left to it for long, they would go wild, though a simple handful

of corn will bring them back within our realm.
How much slowness
must be reabsorbed then, upon reentry, letting the quickness
out as the fat flies do

slowing down now that they've come, at last, to live indoors,
connecting station to station
in one last map. To be saved
is to keep finding new solutions to the problem, like scat

singing or improvisation where you're never wrong
as long as you keep on.
Here it is time again to plant tobacco. The men await full moon
then take themselves

naked to the fields.
What they bury there is the domestic. It alone
can tempt a perfectly obedient crop in rows as true as jewels
or the thick hair being cut now by the women knotted indoors,

cut in fullness
for fullness. Imitation is the light
where the everyday becomes a spell—and these mothers
braiding their hair once more into its perennial solution,

cut chord, worry a bit
for their children scrambling up the hills to find the pigs
in time, though how close we can afford to come to losing them
without losing them is the measure

of our fullness, the shadow thinned to nothing, the finished
spell like the pearl
the moonlight is making
from the suffering of an otherwise empty sky.

A FEATHER FOR VOLTAIRE

The bird is an alphabet, it flies
above us, catch
as catch can,
a flock,
a travel plan.
Some never touch ground.

And each flight is an arc to buttress the sky,
a loan to the sky.
And the little words we make of them, the single feathers, dropped
for us to recover,
fall and fall,
a nimble armor . . .

feather feather of this morning where does your garden grow
flying upwind, saying look
it is safe
never to land,
it is better.
A man full of words

is a garden of weeds,
and when the weeds grow,
a garden of snow,
a necklace of tracks: it was here, my snow owl perhaps.
Who scared it away?
I, said the sparrow,

with my need, its arrow. And so here I belong, trespassing, alone,
in this nation of turns
not meant to be taken
I've taken.
A feather,
pulled from the body or found on the snow

can be dipped into ink
to make one or more words: *possessive, the sun.* A pen
can get drunk,
having come so far, having so far to go—*meadow,*
in vain, imagine
the pain

and when he was gone then there was none

and this is the key to the kingdom.

NOTES ON THE POEMS

"Hybrids of Plants and of Ghosts": The title is from a passage in Friedrich Nietzsche's *Thus Spoke Zarathustra*, trans. R. J. Hollingdale, Penguin Classics ed., 1961: "But he who is wisest among you, he also is only a discord and hybrid of plant and of ghost" (p. 42).

"To Paul Eluard": The poem is loosely inspired by Robert Motherwell's book, *The Dada Painters and Poets*, New York, 1951.

"An Artichoke for Montesquieu": Some phrasing is influenced by Archibald MacLeish's *Brothers in the Eternal Cold*.

"Mirrors": The second line is from Hollingdale's translation of Nietzsche, "What can be loved in man is that he is a going-across and a down-going" (*Übergang und Untergang*) (p. 44).

"Syntax": This poem is for Bill Graham.

LIBRARY OF CONGRESS CATALOGING IN PUBLICATION DATA

Graham, Jorie, 1951-
  Hybrids of plants and of ghosts.

  (Princeton series of contemporary poets)
  Poems.
  I. Title.
PS3557.R214H9   811'.54   79-3210
ISBN 0-691-06421-0
ISBN 0-691-01335-7 pbk.